GLOBAL MANAGEMENT JOURNAL

Table of Contents

Table of Contents 1

GLOBAL TALENT CHALLENGES – *Are You Ready?* 5

CREATIVITY AND INNOVATION – *Lessons from Pixar* ..16

GLOBAL BRANDING – *Challenges and Insights* 27

MULTI-GENERATIONAL TALENT MANAGEMENT – *Overcoming the Generational Gap* 39

STRESS AND WORK-LIFE BALANCE – *How do You Measure Up?* 50

CHANGE AND TRANSFORMATION MANAGEMENT – *Managing Change to Secure Success* 59

ASSESSMENT AND DEVELOPMENT CENTRES – *Recruiting for Success* 71

LEADERSHIP – *Arise Aspiring Entrepreneurs* 83

MENTORING MATTERS…COACHING COUNTS 93

STRATEGIC ORGANISATIONAL DEVELOPMENT –
Approaches and Challenges 104

ABOUT THE AUTHOR 115

REFERENCES 118

ACKNOWLEDGEMENTS

I would like to extend my sincere thanks to the following colleagues who have been instrumental in providing me with top class global research and information to enable me to publish this journal. My thanks go to Sarah Garnett, Katherine Andrews, Marjory Wright, Zsofia Hankó, Klaudia Darbinova and Michal Bardo from the Manchester Research Group.

INTRODUCTION

I am very happy to present this new Global Management Journal which covers a variety of topics under the category of business and people management with a global context. The journal will provide the reader with a robust understanding of all the key activities involved in managing global organisations today and maintaining high performance, including chapters on multi-generational talent management, leadership, creativity and innovation and managing change. I hope reading this journal will bring as much pleasure to you as it has brought to me in thoroughly framing and amalgamating it. I would value your inputs for making this endeavour an accomplishment for us and we look forward to your comments and suggestions here at Michael A Potter International on info@map-int.com.

GLOBAL TALENT CHALLENGES – *Are You Ready?*

Despite the continuing caution exercised by many organisations in the midst of ongoing economic uncertainty, the race for talent, more commonly known as the 'war for talent' still remains a significant feature of the global economy. Therefore, employers all over the globe must implement appropriate recruitment, development and retention strategies in order to engage in the ultimate race for talent and succeed.

Talented personnel can enrich performance and drive a business forward. Thus it is essential that organisations select the right candidates and nurture their skills for the future.

Is there a Talent Shortage?

According to the recent Manpower Talent Shortage Survey (2015), globally one in three (38%) employers reported experiencing a lack of qualified job applicants. This is an

increase from 36% in 2014 and is a three percentage point rise from 2013 (35%) – and also the highest level in eight years. While the global economic downturn may have disguised the talent shortage for several years, the global recovery has made the pressures of the talent shortage more evident as organisations that cut back on staff are discovering that they need more of the right people in place to move forward and support their business strategy.

The primary reasons cited for talent shortages in the Manpower survey include a lack of necessary experience, environmental/market factors such as lack of available talent, and lack of technical competencies, business knowledge and formal qualifications. This suggests that employers need to seriously re-evaluate their recruitment strategies to ensure that they are looking in the right talent pools and are using appropriate techniques to reach candidates.

A Strategy for Success

Recruiting Talent

The recruitment stage is the first step towards creating a talented workforce and selecting your stars of the future. It is difficult to discern the origins of talent; therefore, organisations must be careful not to be influenced by preconceived notions of talent attributed to education or a privileged upbringing. Talent can come in all shapes and sizes, thus it is important to explore a diverse applicant pool.

Recruitment and selection is a process used for predicting the potential job performance of the applicants. The difference between traditional and competency-based recruitment and selection is that the latter concentrates more on formal, measurable competencies. During the competency-based interview assessors would focus on asking the candidates behaviour-type questions instead of probing about hypothetical situations. This gives candidates an opportunity to provide real life examples from their professional experience which can be used as evidence that the candidate has required competencies for the position. The required competencies must also be aligned with the company's future objectives to ensure there is a good fit between the employees and the organisation.

Further to competency-based interviews the assessment centre method is now increasingly being used as a tool to recruit the right talent. The assessment centre method involves multiple evaluation techniques, including various types of job related simulations, and sometimes interviews and psychological tests. The main advantage of using the assessment centre method is that it allows employers to assess and review exactly how an individual would behave in a given task and measure competencies associated with the job. It also has the advantage of assessing many candidates at one time, saving time and money.

 **Recruitment at Virgin**

When Virgin recruit for Cabin Crew, Airport and Contact Centre staff they usually implement an assessment centre consisting of a group discussion, role plays, an analysis presentation, ability tests and a behavioural interview. Although being a nerve-shattering experience for the candidates, it is one of the most efficient methods of recruitment.

Developing Talent

Once the candidates have been selected and are employed by the organisation, it is critical that investment in their talents does not come to a halt. Their skills need to be continually nurtured and developed to drive the performance of the organisation.

Successful talent management is achieved by focusing your resources, time and energy on those who are crucial to your organisation's future. A cost-effective method of catering for your employee's development needs is via talent segmentation. It helps an organisation select which employees to focus on.

All employees need support in the form of career guidance and direction. In particular, younger employees would benefit from advice on a variety of career paths to be followed so that they may broaden their perspective on their future career. The desired outcome is that they are able to capitalise on their competencies and progress into a role which truly suits them.

Enlarging and enriching job roles can be achieved by providing employees with more responsibilities, enabling them to be more autonomous in their posts. This way their capabilities can be recognised and they in turn can become more capable individuals. The development of personnel allows skills to be transferable within the entire organisation.

Retaining Talent

The final key stage is to ensure that once employers have invested time and money in their employees, these employees remain at the organisation and stay committed enough to perform that extra mile.

Organisations need to structure themselves in a way that allows individuals to develop and move ahead; otherwise they risk losing their talent to competitors. Organisations need to permit talented personnel a level of autonomy over their work, enabling a feeling of empowerment. This could be achieved by implementing a flatter as opposed to a hierarchical organisational structure.

It is important that personnel are financially rewarded in the form of bonuses or salary promotions. They will feel a sense of recognition, satisfaction and motivation that their good work has been appreciated. However, rewards can be in the form of psychological rewards too, such as making an individual feel valued for their contribution, praising their efforts or allowing them more responsibility. When an individual enters into an employment contract, they also agree to a psychological contract. The organisation imposes upon the individual certain expectations about how they are to be treated. When an organisation treats its employees well, then it is likely that this behaviour will be reciprocated. If this psychological contract is in some way violated, then there is a risk that the personnel will not work to their full potential and decide to leave.

Organisations need to create a supportive working environment and culture. Individuals who have adequate social support from colleagues at work will be more likely to form strong bonds with them, which in turn creates solid ties with the organisations. A key message is that employers must create a working environment where the positive aspects far outweigh those pulling factors that lure talent away from organisations.

Siemens' Talent Management Strategy

German global electronics company Siemens state that "an organisation is nothing without its people"- which is an inspiring message from their talent management strategy.

Siemens aspires to create a culture of excellence through high performance. They believe that people can only achieve high performance if they operate in a culture which supports and nurtures their development so that they may achieve their own personal goals. Siemens feel that their high performance culture provides this. They enable the foundation of employee development, allowing their skills and expertise to flourish through offering them the guidance within a supportive and mutually beneficial culture. It is through meeting personal goals that the individual is best able to help the organisation achieve its targets. The key theme being: if Siemens is committed to its personnel then they will be committed to Siemens (Duff, 2011).

For further information on this issue and how your organisation can take the next steps towards developing an effective talent management system, Michael A. Potter International runs his World Series Paper: Global Talent Management: Recruitment, Retention & Development

"Strategies for the Future" as a workshop at internationally recognised conferences and events throughout the world.

Key Learning Points

- Organisations must remain flexible to be able to adapt to the fluid changes of the market.
- There is a global talent shortage, with a 3% rise in 2015 (Manpower, 2015).
- Recruitment, Development and Retention are the key strategies to remain ahead in the race for talent.

Useful Hints and Tips

- Use competency-based interviews in the recruitment process.
- Encourage younger employees to broaden their perspective of possible career choices.

- Be more open when recruiting talent; do not be afraid to take someone who is less capable but a good learner.
- Ensure that all personnel are developed in order to have necessary skills and competencies to succeed as managers.
- Use various types of reward to prevent talented personnel from leaving.

CREATIVITY AND INNOVATION – Lessons from Pixar

It is no secret to anyone that creativity plays a critical role in the innovation process, and innovation that markets value is a creator and sustainers of performance and change. Companies that are trying to make their organisations more innovative can derive inspiration from organisations such as Pixar - the animation film studio. Pixar's laid back management style which encourages child-like creativity and innovation from staff is a benchmark for organisations wishing to enhance creativity and innovation in their employees (Catmull, 2008).

The Need for Creativity and Innovation

For an organisation to be competitive it needs to continually adapt to new situations which requires innovation. This is especially true when economic pressure is high. The best way for an organisation to gain competitive edge is through the innovation of its people. A competitor can copy other aspects of an organisation such as products and services, but it cannot

copy an organisation's people. In today's businesses an employee's values may lie in their potential for innovation and the creation of new knowledge. An employee's potential for innovation however is dependent upon many factors, but creativity is always a prerequisite. Innovation is the implementation of new and useful ideas, but these ideas have to come from somewhere and creativity is the process through which ideas are developed.

It is safe to say that Pixar is a pace setter when it comes to innovation. Pixar ensures innovation of its staff by providing a culture and outlet where staff can release creativity without bounds.

Creativity, Innovation and Employees

There is an inaccurate notion that creativity is innate; that some people are born as 'creative' and others are not. Anyone can be creative if given the right tools and environment to encourage it. People who naturally tend to be less creative can be influenced by external factors and become more creative. An employee's personal characteristics interact with contextual factors such as working culture and management style to determine creative performance. Those with the greatest personal creativity combined with the optimum working context will potentially produce the most innovative ideas, and even those with low personal creative characteristics when provided with the optimum working context will produce significant creative ideas.

Creativity and Innovation in Practice

Although the subject of individual creativity is an important one, an employee being creative in isolation may not be advantageous to the organisation. Good ideas may go unheard, misunderstood or may be deemed unsuitable even when they simply require some development or input by others. Alternatively many employees may spend time developing the same idea which could result in 'reinventing the wheel' and the workforce as a whole would not be producing innovative ideas. This highlights the need for a process of openness and good communication, seated within the organisational context of 'creative culture'.

Pixar co-founder Ed Catmull says employees must be linked not ranked. Pixarians are linked together by complimentary skills, not ranked by level of importance. *"When art and technology come together, magical things happen"* (Ed Catmull, 2008).

Corporate innovation relies on a number of factors including the corporate recognition that creativity is everyone's business; the existence of a culture of cross functional team working, the ability of managers to sponsor innovation, and the openness of the organisation to absorb ideas from all sources. An organisation is only innovative if it allows its employees to be creative, and the leadership structure is supportive of this process. Innovation is a result of the creative management of human capital.

The importance of team working and being open to all ideas has been expressed in a quote from Brad Bird, one of the directors at Pixar, during an interview with 'The Quarterly':

'I got everybody in a room. This was different from what the previous guy had done; he had reviewed the work in private,

generated notes, and sent them to the person.... I said, look, this is a young team. As individual animators, we all have different strengths and weaknesses, but if we can interconnect all our strengths, we are collectively the greatest animator on earth. So I want you guys to speak up and drop your drawers. We're going to look at your scenes in front of everybody. Everyone will get humiliated and encouraged together...' (Rao et al. 2008)

Creative ideas come from team work, not top-down instructions. For example, Ed Catmull disagrees with many of his counterparts in Hollywood studios who insist that Pixar and Disney have all the "great idea people." *"It is not about great ideas... it is all about great teams"*. Ed's belief in his team is evident in his words:

"If you give a good idea to a mediocre team, they'll screw it up. But if you give a mediocre idea to a great team, they'll make it work."

It is not about one great idea; it is about the thousands of little ideas that come from everyone on the team that go into the final product.

Employees need to have the opportunity and resources to experiment freely in order to develop skills such as playfulness, creative perception and exploration of various options. Creativity is largely conducted through a trial and error technique, so employees need to develop the skills required to carry out that method. They need to break out of developed performance scripts to perceive things differently, to be playful and make wild suggestions, then be open to the usefulness of all suggestions but also be prepared to fail. Making mistakes is part of the creative thinking skills required, as it is important to learn from what has not worked and analyse why, with an open mind, in order to utilise this information within the creative process.

7 Creative Problem Solving Techniques

1. Take note of assumptions and constraints with the problem. Often, these assumptions can obstruct our view of possible solutions. Note which assumptions are not valid and which need to be addressed.

2. Take a hard look at what the problem really is. Know the problem and have a concrete understanding of what it is about. By knowing what the problem is and how it works, you may find that you will have built a better foundation towards solving the problem. Identify all the participating entities and then decide what their relationship is to one another. Take a note of all the things you stand to gain or lose due to the current problem. Once you have considered the following you should have a clear and simple statement of what the problem is.

3. Try solving the problem in parts. For example, going from the more general views to the more detailed parts of the

problem may help solve it. This method is called the top down approach. First, write down a question and then come up with a general one-sentence solution. Now you will be able to develop the solution even further.

4. It is important to keep a creative and analytical voice of reason at the back of your head. If someone else suggests a solution, be creative; think of how to make the solution work. Also think realistically and look for any possible weak links in the suggested solution.

5. Remain open-minded to the fact that there may be more than one solution to the problem. Keep track of them and go with the one that best fits your situation.

6. You know the old saying, "two heads are better than one." It is very true, so remember to be open to new ideas. There may be answers for problems that you thought were unsolvable. You will benefit from listening to others, especially when the information is coming from someone who has had experience with a similar problem to yours.

> 7. Be patient. There is always a chance that a solution will present itself. Remember, no one is able to come up with the right invention the first time around.

Brad Bird acknowledges the importance of giving employees opportunity to explore and experiment by saying:

'If you walk around downstairs in the animation area, you'll see that it is unhinged. People are allowed to create whatever front to their office they want. One guy might build a front that's like a Western town. Someone else might do something that looks like Hawaii...John [Lasseter] believes that if you have a loose, free kind of atmosphere, it helps creativity.'

He also highlighted the importance of developing the skills of employees by saying:

'One thing Pixar does is "PU," or Pixar University. If you work in lighting but you want to learn how to animate, there's a class to show you animation. There are classes in story structure, in Photoshop, even in Krav Maga, the Israeli self-defence system. Pixar basically encourages people to learn

outside their areas, which makes them more creative.'

Therefore one can see that management at Pixar is dedicated to bringing out creativity and innovation in employees.

Key Learning Points

- In order to remain competitive, organisations need to remain creative and innovative.
- When the right environment is provided employees who tend to be less creative can produce creative ideas.
- Open communication and team work are essential for fostering creative and innovative cultures.
- Employees can have their skills developed through training to further develop their creative abilities.

 **Useful Hints and Tips**

- Try and build a culture that fosters creativity by ensuring open communication, freedom to experiment, teamwork and adequate training for employees.
- Encourage a fun office environment where employees are not scared to make wild and 'outside the box' suggestions.
- Always acknowledge the fact that although an employee may seem less creative, their creative abilities can be developed if the culture of the firm allows it.
- Make use of techniques such as the problem solving techniques listed above to help the harness creativity in your organisation.

GLOBAL BRANDING – Challenges and Insights

What is Branding?

A brand is the public perception of a business, product or service – in other words, its reputation. Today, the concept of branding is being embraced, not only by large corporations, but by individuals and small businesses.

How Is A Good Brand Beneficial?

Having a good brand image is beneficial in a number of ways. Initially, successful branding will create a good public image. When people hear of the business, a good brand means that it will be envisaged in a positive light. A successful brand will ensure your company is considered favourably, which will assist in helping to build your credibility and ultimately have more influence within the market. Consequently, this will encourage the use of your services or purchase of your products which will boost sales and eventually, profit. Furthermore, potential employees will wish to join your organisation, creating a wide pool of candidates for job vacancies, ensuring the best selection of employees.

How Is A Brand Created?

The ultimate purpose of branding is to create confidence in your business. However, developing an effective brand requires time and patience, both in the creation and implementation phases. A brand cannot be created overnight - it has to be planned, maintained and groomed. Time, money and energy will be wasted without planning. However, when done effectively, the process is worth it.

What is critical to effective brand management is a clear definition of the objectives that the brand needs to achieve. To determine your brand objectives the following questions need to be considered, 'What do you want your brand to do for your company?' and 'What do you want others to know and say about your products or services?'.

The next stage is to build and develop your brand strategy. This can be achieved by creating a list of how, when and what can be done in order to meet the proposed brand objectives. Initially, a SWOT Analysis should be conducted, evaluating the Strengths, Weaknesses, Opportunities and Threats of the product. During this, it is necessary to be honest, as exaggeration of any success will not help to create a successful brand. Next, the product should be reviewed, describing what it does, why it exists, its benefits and how it differs from competition. Throughout the brainstorming session, ideas should not be easily rejected as ridiculous, as these often have practical applications.

The list should be reduced down to the three best ideas. A focus group should then be gathered to determine the reactions, perceptions, misconceptions, feelings and general opinion of each idea. Another focus group made up of staff, board members and current customers should be used then.

At a minimum, the member's opinions should guide the final branding statement. A descriptive statement, around one to two paragraphs should embody who the company is and what it uniquely delivers. These sentences or short phrases that each member says about the business should be remembered. These could become useful later.

Once the best idea is identified, you should decide what information needs to be conveyed and to whom. Using specific time limits, it is easier to create the plan of action which will help to achieve the objectives. Once all this information has been decided, the marketing departments can ensure the message is relayed to the relevant parties as best and as soon as possible. As the brand is implemented, it is crucial that everyone affiliated with the business is able to articulate the messages. Every person who represents the company is a brand ambassador, from the CEO to the receptionist.

How Can A Brand Be Represented?

Once the brand is identified, the visual and textual elements, such as name, logo and slogan can be designed. These should reflect the brand's character and values, as well as matching the interests and lifestyles of the target audience.

The first stage of representing a brand is to identify a name. These include:

- Acronym such as IBM,
- Description of the product like Airbus,
- Alliteration, which sticks in the mind like Dunkin' Donuts,
- Evocative, evoking a vivid image such as Amazon,
- Neologism, which is a completely made-up word, like Wii.

A brand can be represented by a logo. Logos should be simple and relate to the organisation. Consistency in the design, including the colour is vital. A logo must be able to speak for itself; it should not need to be explained.

While creating a logo is a critical stage in brand development, it should be remembered that your logo is not your brand.

Visual elements represent the brand and have the ability to play a key role in identifying an emotional connection with the product or service. For example, an apple bitten into for

'Apple', a simple yellow 'M' for 'McDonalds', five coloured connecting rings for the 'Olympics' and a swoosh tick for 'Nike'.

Once a logo is created it is crucial that it becomes integrated into all corporate communication, in order for it to gain maximum exposure. So this would include advertisements, brochures, letter heads, your website and all media relations. This is fundamental to build a successful brand identity.

A logo should be used for at least twenty years. If this seems like a long time, consider the fact that you are more likely to become bored of your logo quicker than others. A change of logo can destroy brand image, therefore it should only be changed for strong reason, such as when the current logo no longer represents your company. However, if and when you fancy a change, an updated version of the logo can be produced, with only small distinctions from the current version. If continuity is evident the logo will still be recognisable.

A brand can be represented by a slogan. A slogan should be developed to define the business to its audience. When heard, it should be immediately associated with the company. When someone says, "The happiest place on earth," your first thought is Disneyland. Other slogans include Nikes "Just do it" and Coco-Cola's "it's always the real thing".

There are a number of ways to develop a successful slogan. They should be uncomplicated and easy to remember. They should be short, as they are typically incorporated into the logo designs, as well as all collateral marketing pieces.

A brand can also be represented by a sound. According to a study conducted by Buyology Incorporated, sound is just as important as sight. They suggest that the most successful brand sound is that of Intel's. Their sound has become so well recognised that it now forms part of their advertising campaign.

How Not To Brand

Sometimes, brands evoke negative connotations. In the past, for example, Starbucks and BP were being accused of acting unethically. As a result of this, consumers and clients were turning elsewhere. Eventually, both companies had to change their Corporate Social Responsibility strategies in order to revoke their images and perceptions, back to the ethical and professional organisations they once had been.

Recent analysts reports, coverage in the major media and the Twitter sphere are being less than kind to Netflix and its two recent corporate announcements: raising prices by 60 percent; and coming back two months later to apologise while announcing the split of the company into two (Netflix and Qwikster). When looking at it from a strategic planning and PR perspective, the best companies incorporate image as a part of corporate strategy, especially when one has

built such a strong brand. They do things right and also do the right things (Dawson, 2012).

Netflix appears to have advanced toward bursting its own brand bubble through eight easy steps:

1. Raised prices seemingly without much consideration for the existing customer base, their needs, wants, and expectations.
2. Went for a big number rather than incremental increases.
3. Provided a rationale that didn't ring true and made many long-term customers feel betrayed by the brand.
4. Did it all top down and one-way in a CEO voice rather than human voice.
5. Didn't join the conversation; didn't use social media to actively engage its many audiences.
6. Waited a couple of months to apologise and then did it with an astonishing lack of sincerity.
7. Seemingly as an afterthought, changed a successful business model to one that confuses customers,

> analysts, and the stock market.
> 8. Gave competitors openings to attack, reposition the company, and declare pricing advantages (Gable, 2012).

If we know how a good brand can be damaged, we can avoid this from occurring.

So What Should We Do With Our Brand?

In summary:

1. Always act in accordance with your organisation's aims
2. Practice your morals
3. Don't be seen to be acting unethically

 **Key Learning Points**

- A good brand can be beneficial to a company in a number of ways, such as to attract more consumers and potential employees.

- Creating a good brand can be a lengthy process; however it is worth the effort in the end.

- There are various methods of representing a brand and a company should choose one that best fits the brands personality and values, as well as matching the interests and lifestyles of the target audience.

- As well as studying good ways of branding, it is important to be aware of branding mistakes and these should be avoided at all costs.

Useful Hints and Tips

- Before embarking on the process of creating or revamping a brand, a thorough planning process should take place.

- Always ensure that people in the organisation are familiar with the brand and have similar values that the brand represents as they are ambassadors of the brand.

- Ensure representations of brands such as slogans or logos are short, precise and easy to remember.

- Study common branding mistakes by popular companies in order to ensure your company doesn't go down the same route.

MULTI-GENERATIONAL TALENT MANAGEMENT – *Overcoming the Generational Gap*

Western countries, including UK, USA and Canada, have already focused research efforts on studying multi-generational diversity in organisations. They have categorised generations using a widely accepted practitioner classification based on birth years related to significant events in history in the western context. The categories so defined are: Veterans, born between 1925 and 1945; Baby Boomers, born between 1946 and 1964; Gen X, born between 1965 and 1977; Gen Y born between 1978 and 1999; and Gen Z, born 2000 and after.

The Generational Gap

The entrance of generation Y and Z into the labour market has and will create a change not only in the age of the labour force, but also in values and preferences when it comes to career and working life. The millennial generations, Generation Y and Z, are able to integrate technology into every aspect of their work whereas older generations in general are not as familiar with technology which could lead to a generation gap. The lack of emerging technologies in the workplace and varying perspectives of different generations have led to a rift between employers and employees and managers are finding it hard to engage millennial generations who are mostly entry level employees leading to a high employee turnover in many organisations. Organisations need to learn how to actively engage the millennials while ensuring that the needs of the older generations are not neglected in the process.

Attracting and Retaining Generation Y and Z

According to the recent study conducted by Price Waterhouse Cooper (2011), millennial generations want more work life balance options such as flexi-time. There is a strong emphasis on balanced work ethics; millennials have good educations thus they are demanding for more flexible work patterns. This leads to recruitment challenges of matching more home-oriented candidates with more firm-oriented work roles. Companies that consider the needs of this generation will be able to attract competent management and good employees and be able to retain them.

Millennial generations also want to work with companies that are well positioned globally, thus companies that concentrate on branding and corporate recognition through peer networks instead of traditional advertising, will be attractive to this age group.

To millennial generations, e-mail is a slow and inefficient tool that is used for communication at work. To attract generation Y and Z, organisations must learn how to adapt new ways to communicate and attract candidates. If organisations are not going social, they will not get the best talents. Building a community around your brand and its values will help to engage these new talents. Organisations should use YouTube, use humour, and go viral with their recruitment efforts.

To attract and retain Gen Y and Z management is expected to communicate with employees in a more relaxed environment through social media. Communication must be interactive and two-way. Companies that hope to be attractive employers may need to change their management and communication structures. Other management structures, such as the virtual office may flow more easily with new organisations rather than those already established. Social media is becoming a major part of the way candidates receive information, thus organisations need to take this seriously to be noticed by the new generations.

Corporate Social Responsibility will continue to be a major issue, with a lot more emphasis on CSR, and the eco-awareness that began in the late 1990's. These generations are looking for a micro-level approach to a green workplace where they can actively contribute within the company. They desire an organised sense of belonging and inclusion – reflected in areas such as personalised workstations. One of the keys to being attractive to the millennial generations is to be a lifelong learner. The days of thinking "school is for learning and work is for working" are gone. Organisations can set their company apart from the competition by being at the top of hiring young talent before everyone else figures it out.

Nokia's Case

With nearly 13 million fans on Facebook, 291,000 followers on Twitter and a prolific output of videos on YouTube, the mobile telecoms group Nokia is a company that seems to know what makes Generation Y tick.

But the world's largest maker of mobile phones doesn't just use social media to promote its products. Sites like Facebook, Twitter and LinkedIn are an important recruiting tool and a way for Nokia to identify its future employees. It has a Facebook group called Future Talent at Nokia ('liked' by 47,000 + people) where recruiters answer questions about working at the company, post information about job and internship opportunities and provide interview tips.

"We want to have a conversation with them," says Matthew Hanwell, HR director, communities and social media at Nokia. "It's not the usual post-and-pray approach to recruitment. This is much more about developing and evolving a relationship with people that ultimately could become an employment relationship."

Nokia's easy rapport with Generation Y – the brand-conscious, technologically-savvy and highly-networked generation of workers born in or after 1980 – is no accident. Since they entered the workforce, Nokia, which defines Generation Y as those born between 1978 and 2000, has paid more and more attention to them, says Hanwell. It has tried not only to understand what makes them different but also how they will shape their workplaces. Already, they make up between 30 and 40 percent of Nokia's global workforce if factory workers are included, and the average age of the Finnish company's employees is just under 33 years. "Over the last few years we have taken this topic very seriously and we have been actively researching and participating in research around Generation Y," Hanwell says. "They are the future of the workforce of every company."

Matthew Hanwell at Nokia encourages CFOs to follow his company's example by having an open culture and engaging with their team. Nokia tries to create a "Generation Y-friendly

environment," he says, supporting things like flexible working and using social media tools within the company that allow employees to engage with senior executives. There is also an open door policy at Nokia and the CEO doesn't have an office. The CEO at Nokia also ensures he is constantly in touch with employees through means such as social media forums.

In 2008, the company ran a reverse mentoring programme in its services unit, in which young engineers were paired with senior management and coached them on how to use social media platforms.

Future Challenges for HR in Managing a Multi-Generational Workplace

Despite the fact that organisations can identify means to manage multi generational environments, it is important to note some of the potential future challenges. One potential challenge may be the process of replacing the Baby Boomers. As the Baby Boomers approach retirement age, companies need to start thinking about their replacement. However, the number of millennial generations may not be sufficient to fill their shoes. Other possible challenges are the process of matching management styles to generational patterns and accommodating different generational needs. This may prove to be difficult and costly as there are several generations to satisfy, so organisations need to find a balance with regards to the leadership styles managers adopt. The different generations present in the workplace will most likely lead to some conflict between them, thus another future challenge for organisations may be managing cross-generational conflict. This may cost managers substantial time and effort that could have been put into productive work.

Potential Solutions to These Future Challenges

One of the most important things managers have to do is ensure that they are aware of the differences between generations. This can be a preventative method, because they can be proactive to prevent the possible challenges previously discussed from occurring. For example, the management styles in organisations can constantly be reviewed to ensure that the

needs of the generations in the firm are always being met. It is also important that employees learn about differences present in the firm. This may make them more understanding about the challenges the organisation faces and may prevent future conflicts in the long run. Organisations should ensure that they have communication strategies such as open door policies in place. This will help employees feel comfortable about voicing any concerns they have and will mean that those concerns can be addressed faster. The organisation can also tailor things to suit individual employees, such as compensation packages and individual development plans. This will further ensure that all the needs of different employees are being met.

Key Learning Points

- In today's day and age, if organisations want to remain competitive, they have to invest in their best asset – their talent.
- Different generations have different needs in the workplace and it is important that organisations continuously adapt to meet the changing needs of upcoming generations.

Useful Hints and Tips

- Try and ensure the needs of each generation present in your organisation are accommodated for. The needs of younger generations can be met through things like ensuring the company is up to date with technology and work practices such as flexi-time. The older generations can be trained on any new technology or work practice that is brought into the organisation to ensure that their needs are not sacrificed.
- Avoid traditional methods of advertising your firm and opt for more modern methods such as peer networks in order to successfully attract the newer generations.

STRESS AND WORK-LIFE BALANCE – *How do You Measure Up?*

Every day millions of employees all over the globe follow the same daily routine: they wake up, go to work, perform their duties, and return back home. These people often find themselves bored, tired and lacking any enthusiasm - sounds familiar? If so, the chances are you might be stressed out!

Stress can be defined as any physical, chemical or emotional factor that causes unrest and is known to be one of the major factors contributing to poor health. Of course not all stress is harmful. Some medium tension can often be very beneficial for us as employees by keeping us focused and motivated at our workplace. However, when badly managed, stress can cause symptoms such as loss of concentration, anxiety, headaches and loss of appetite. In addition, prolonged stress may cause the feeling of being "burned-out" as well as loss of

interest in normal activities. (Management Systems Asia, Dec 2009).

According to the Chartered Institute of Personnel and Development (CIPD) stress-related illness is the top cause of long-term absence in Europe and is a factor in 50 - 60 % of all lost working days. However stressed employees often choose not to consult with their managers or visit a doctor because they are afraid to lose their jobs. Therefore, it has become very challenging for the management to identify individuals who are most exposed to the problem. These situations cause not only illnesses but also serious financial problems for organisations. For example, 4% of EU's GDP is lost due to stress related absence each year with UK companies loosing up to £673 annually.

What can companies do to stop this?

There are many different strategies that organisations can adopt in order to help their employees reduce stress and optimise their work-life balance.

One of the methods could be to improve employees' entertainment. For example, one of the top media agencies in London uses a scheme in which employees can claim up to £150 per year to start "after work activities". The main condition is that those activities should not be related to daily work routine but should rather provide employees with a new skill. The most popular examples for such "after work activities" are language courses, photography and sea kayaking.

Organisations also need to ensure that enough time is allocated to employees to complete their tasks and that good mental health is promoted at all time. For example, many companies offer gym or yoga activities during lunchtime hours to help employees reduce their stress. Another good example is Oasis of Calm (Figure 1). Such room for prayers and reflection are still a rare view in Europe, but apart from having a religious function Oasis of Calm can also serve as a place where people can contemplate and de-stress.

Figure 1: St Ethelburga's interfaith tent. Source: People Management, December 2011

Part-time working hours are becoming more and more popular among the top management in Europe. Professionals who choose this new trend of employment usually work 3 to 4 days per week. This has both, advantages and drawbacks. Helen Michaels, a global innovation director of the multinational drinks firm Diageo, switched to part time hours 7 years ago after managing to negotiate the flexible hours with her boss to become a mum (People Management, November 2012). However, she admits that her flexible working hours have come at the expense of her career progression which over the years has slowed down dramatically. Nevertheless, part-time work can provide the means to keep talented individuals in the workplace, especially women who are shown to be more likely to give up their careers once they start a family (Figure 2).

With the new Generation Y now entering the workforce and Generation Z not far behind companies seriously need to rethink their work-life balance strategies in order to attract and retain the new talent. According to the PWC *Managing Tomorrow's People* survey current Generation Ys already prioritise flexible working hours and work-life balance over cash bonuses, which mean that companies have to start moving towards rewarding by results rather than by number of hours worked.

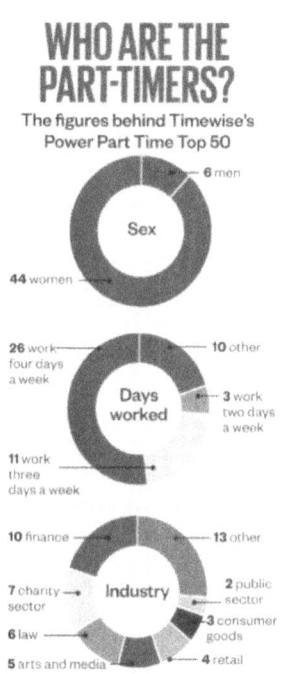

Figure 2: Who are the part-timers? Source: People Management, December 2012

According to OECD "Better Life index" Poland is on the 28th place among 36 OECD states in terms of Work-Life Balance. On average people in Poland work 1,939 hours a year in comparison to the OECD average of 1,749 hours. This situation is a potential threat as to reduce work-related stress it is better to adopt a culture of "working smart, not long", working from home or sharing jobs. The more people work, the less time they have to spend on other activities, such as spending time with family and friend or on leisure activities. People in Poland devote 66% of their day, or 14.2 hours, to personal care (eating, sleeping, etc.) and leisure (socialising, entertainment, sports) – close to the OECD average of 14.8 hours which proves that despite long working hours Polish people don't neglect their after work life.

We all need to work to earn means to live, to gain satisfaction and to increase our self esteem, but we shouldn't work too hard or long as it may lead to stress, "burnout" and as a result health problems. The amount and quality of leisure time is important for our overall well-being, and can bring additional physical and mental health benefits. Let's remember that each of us has many more decades to work, so let's plan this time wisely to have a happy, healthy working life,

 **Key Learning Points**

- Stress is one of the major factors contributing to poor health. Loss of concentration, anxiety, headaches and loss of appetite are all symptoms of being stressed.
- One of the biggest challenges for managers is to identify stressed employees as employees are often to worried about losing their job and do not notify their managers about their stress-related issues.
- Fun after-work activities and physical fitness can contribute to reducing your employees stress levels.
- Flexible working hours are becoming a priority for the new Generation Y.

GLOBAL MANAGEMENT JOURNAL

Useful Hints and Tips

- Work-life balance is important. To keep stress-free employees must be able to switch off at the end of the day and carry out their personal life activities.

- Encourage employees to keep fit by providing gym facilities and yoga classes.

- Allow employees to work part-time hours where possible. This will help to reduce their levels of stress and improve their motivation and performance.

CHANGE AND TRANSFORMATION MANAGEMENT – *Managing Change to Secure Success*

The Need for Change

The rate and scope of global change has led to the need for companies to be resilient, innovative and adaptive in order to survive in today's dynamic business environment. Change management has been recognised as an important catalyst in reaching business goals and creating cultures of high performance in the current business climate. For example, Nokia has continually adapted to its changing environment by transforming from a pulp and paper mill in 1865 to the cellular telephone company it is today. Nokia executives sensed the emerging market for wireless communication and effective change management helped them achieve success.

Effective Change and Transformational Management

In a study done by the Hay Group in 2014 it was found that 30% of all change initiatives fail to reach expectations mainly due to HRM issues. This finding shows that the study of effective change management in the context of HRM is essential.

Lewin's Change Management Model

This model consists of 3 stages which can be practically applied by companies.

Unfreeze

This first stage of change involves preparing the organisation to accept that change is necessary, which involves breaking down the existing status quo before building up a new way of operating.

Change

After the uncertainty created in the unfreeze stage, the change stage is where people begin to resolve their uncertainties and look for new ways to do things. People start to believe and act

in ways that support the new direction.

Refreeze

When the changes are taking shape and people have embraced the new ways of working, the organisation is ready to refreeze. The outward signs of the refreeze are a stable organisation chart and consistent job descriptions (and so on). The refreeze stage also needs to help people and the organisation internalise or institutionalise the changes.

Continental Airlines

From poorest performing airline to airline of the year

The application of Lewin's Change model can be seen clearly in the huge transformation of Continental Airlines from the poorest performing airline to the airline of the year.

Reasons for change in Continental Airlines

Continental Airlines had a rocky history staring in the 80's when it filed for bankruptcy which led to it being taken over by Texas Air Corp. After several mergers that led to the increase of their aircraft inventory and their routes, Continental Airlines continued to fail. They filed for bankruptcy again in 1990.

Application of Lewin's Change model

Unfreezing

In 1994 Gordon Bethune (Bethune) took over the failing company and immediately began the unfreezing process. He began to break the failing system while still maintaining order. He did this by transitioning the company's focus from cost savings to putting out a quality product based on the standards of customers.

Change

During this phase Bethune offered recognition and rewards for company improvement. For example if the US department of transportation put Continental Airlines as one of the top 5 airlines, the employees would receive $65 and if not, no one

would receive any bonuses. This led to cohesiveness in the company as everyone succeeded or failed together. Gordon Bethune was also open and honest with staff throughout the change process which led to cohesiveness.

Refreezing

Once the changes and employees settled, Bethune was able to refreeze the organisation making the changes permanent. Continental still focuses on customer needs today which shows Bethune's successful implementation of organisational change.

Barriers and Resistance to Change

There are several reasons why change may be resisted in an organisation. These can be split into organisational resistance and individual resistance. Some examples of reasons for organisational resistance are threat to established power relationship and failure of previous change initiatives. Some individual reasons for resistance include habit, fear of the unknown, misunderstanding and low tolerance of change.

Overcoming Barriers and Resistance to Change

Some ways of minimising resistance to change include communication with employees on issues relating to change. The key elements in effective communication of a vision are said to be

- Simplicity – eliminate complicated terms
- Metaphor, analogy and example – to help illustrate points
- Multiple Forums – in order to ensure that every employee is reached and connected with
- Repetition – similar to the idea of 'practice makes perfect'
- Leadership by Example – 'do as I do' not necessarily 'do as I say'. Management have to practice what they preach.
- Explain inconsistencies – in order to reduce doubts staff have
- Give and take – two way communication is very important.

Employees also need to be trained on key areas that the change process will affect in order for them to possess the required competences to help build their confidence and overcome resistance to change. Employees should also be involved in

activities relating to the change process in order for them to have a sense of belonging.

Corus Strip Products UK (A subsidiary of Tata Steel)

Corus Strip Products UK (CSP UK) is a subsidiary of Tata Steel which manufactures, processes and distributes steel and aluminium products and services to companies around the world. In 2005, CSP UK introduced a cultural plan for change which would address several business challenges with a central theme of the way employees at all levels went about their work.

Barriers To Change in CSP UK

CSP was an established business in a traditional industry; thus there was a set way of doing things and an attitude of 'this is the way we do things around here'. This made it difficult to implement necessary changes. There was a fear of the unknown possessed by some CSP UK employees and they saw the proposed new initiatives as threats to their existing positions and teams. Some of CSP UK's previous change initiatives had led to job cuts and this led to complacency in the staff that remained in the organisation because they felt untouchable. This complacency was a barrier to change in CSP UK.

One of the main techniques CSP UK used to overcome these barriers was to work closely with employees and to get them involved as much as possible in the programme. The company also ensured they constantly communicated with the staff.

Involving Employees

CSP UK ensured everyone took ownership of the new values by getting them to physically sign up for the programme. Workers were also more involved in decision making and their contributions were recognised through workshops for example. Weaknesses of the plan were also shown to employees and they were encouraged to make changes.

Communication

There were fortnightly newspapers and about 150 workshops that highlighted the new values of CSP UK. There were also repeated key messages through articles on various issues such as employees taking part in redesigning of a certain control room. Intranet, Billboards and one-to-one conversations all reinforced the messages.

Training

Employees were also trained and assisted in order to improve their performance. This led to fewer mistakes on the part of the employees. These techniques helped ensure effective change management in CSP UK (The Times 100 Business Case Studies (2012).

Monitoring the Change Process

It is imperative that the change process is monitored throughout in order to gain focus, direction and momentum. When doing this it may be useful to have a set of questions similar to a checklist in order to ensure key areas have been covered. Some of these questions are:

1. Have we stated our objectives in concrete terms?
2. Have we translated these objectives to observable behaviours?
3. Have we set milestones that all understand and agree to?
4. Are expected results tied to external and internal goals and have we ensured that outcomes will be evident to stakeholders?
5. Are individuals and teams accountable for results?
6. Do we know which existing data will pick up progress toward our goal?
7. Have we established new ways to gather data?
8. Do we have accurate and timely baseline data to work from?

Key Learning Points

- Companies can practically apply theoretical models such as Lewin's Change model in order to help with the change management process.
- Various organisational factors such as threat to established power relationships and individual factors such as fear of the unknown can be barriers to effective change management.
- These barriers can be overcome through processes such as communication, training and employee involvement.
- The change process can be effectively monitored by using sets of questions that are similar to a checklist.

 Useful Hints and Tips

- Organisations should ensure they are always adapting to suit the dynamic business climates.
- Companies should not see barriers to change as a dead end, but should constantly look for ways to overcome these barriers.
- It should be ensured that employees are kept in the loop throughout the whole change process in order to prevent resistance to change.
- Managers should ensure the messages they try and pass across to employees are simple and repeated numerous times in order to ensure coherence.

ASSESSMENT AND DEVELOPMENT CENTRES – *Recruiting for Success*

The term 'Assessment and Development Centre' refers to a recruitment process, as opposed to a physical place. Traditionally, the process is undertaken by the top applicants for a vacancy and involves partaking in a combination of exercises. All exercises simulate the activities carried out in the job, by measuring a number of pre-defined competencies, skills or personality traits required for the role. The reasoning behind this is that in order to predict future job performance, an individual should carry out a range of exercises which accurately reflect and measure the competencies necessary for the role and are as similar to them as possible.

Exercises can include psychometric tests, individual in-tray exercises, group discussions, role plays, group problem-solving tasks and interviews. Each test is scored by specially trained assessors, who evaluate each participant against the pre-determined criteria.

An Assessment and Development Centre does not last for a pre-defined length of time; it merely has to last for as long as it takes to successfully measure all competencies. All Assessment and Development Centres demand full commitment from the host organisation.

What Are They Used For Today?

Today, Assessment and Development Centres are widely used by companies of all sizes as a key recruiting and selection method, as well as to assess existing staff for training, promotion and development.

Although the term encompasses 'Assessment' and 'Development' Centres, both actually hold different purposes. They both involve assessing candidates, however, the use of the information which is extracted from each day, differs.

Assessment Centres are used purely for selection of new employees, whereas Development Centres involve self-assessment to identify participant's key strengths, as well as areas which they need to work on and develop. However, most

Assessment Centres involve some development and most Development Centres involve some assessment.

It is common practice for an Assessment Centre where the candidates are all internal to the company, to be referred to as a Development Centre, due to the negative connotations of being assessed. Candidates are less likely to feel they are being judged and will view the event in a more positive light and as a way to identify where their strengths lie and how they can improve their weaknesses.

Typically, Assessment Centres:

- Are used in order to fill a job vacancy
- Tend to have external individuals as the candidates
- Address and meet an immediate organisational need
- Use a range of different exercises to measure the required competencies for the role
- Focus on what the candidate can do now
- Have more participants than assessors

- Have a pass/fail outcome
- Give feedback to candidates following the day

Whereas Development Centres:

- Address and meet the longer term needs of the organisation
- Use one assessor per participant
- Are aimed at assisting the individual
- Focus on the potential of the candidate
- Place greater emphasis on self-assessment
- Do not have a pass/fail criteria
- Place emphasis on development feedback
- Tend to give feedback imminently

BT Case Study

The telecommunications company BT wanted to enhance their

business performance. As a result, they conducted an Assessment Centre, attended by 850 managers over a 6-week period. BT believes that a net 10% saving on expenditure is expected, as a result of this Assessment Centre.

The Process

Initially, a job description and person specification for any job vacancy must be compiled. Using the job analysis, the key competencies required to be successful in the role should be identified and exercises must be chosen which will measure these key competencies.

The particular competencies used will depend purely upon the job. However, often, one will find competencies common within a number of roles, such as communication, team-work, adaptability and flexibility, problem-solving, planning and organising, working under pressure and decision-making skills.

A competency matrix should then be designed, which allows a clear indication of which exercises will measure which competencies.

Using a range of tests and a pre-defined scoring system ensures a fair, accurate and objective method of assessment and eliminates any subjective bias of the assessors. It also ensures that selection is not based on whether the individual's face 'fits' with the organisation or because the candidate 'seemed good', but on their behaviour on the Assessment Day and how well they fit with the key competencies of the role. Furthermore, by being judged by more than one assessor, candidates face a more objective assessment of their behaviours.

Recent Surveys

Research shows that a well designed Assessment Centre is the most objective method for observing and systematically measuring how people will perform in reality and it is the most

effective tool for assessing individuals in both individual and group based environments.

Although larger organisations are more likely to use Assessment Centres, according to XpertHR, two-thirds of all employers use this form of selection method.

90.6% of the employers who took part in the XpertHR survey found that candidates generally reacted positively to the

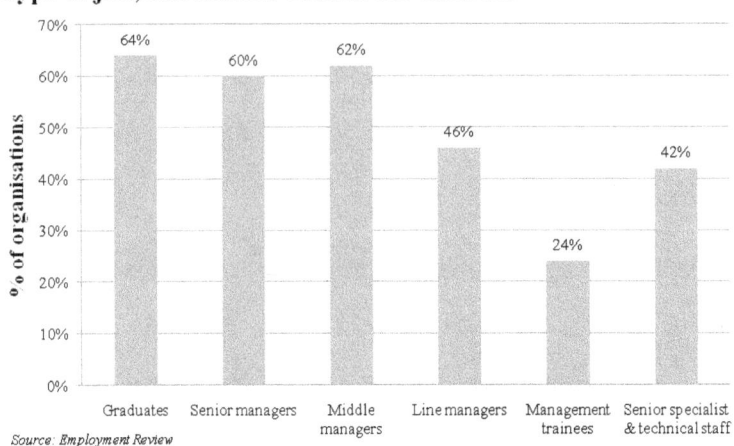

Type of job, assessment centres are used for

Source: Employment Review

experience of taking part in the Assessment Centre. Nine out of ten employers also believe that they are an effective selection process. Most enthusiastic about Assessment Centres were Private Sector companies, with 56% considering them as very effective. Only 47% of Public Sector organisations agreed, but less than one in three manufacturing companies agreed.

Given the potential cost of Assessment Centres, it would be logical to use them for high-value roles, such as more senior or specialist staff or for Graduates who are likely to be future leaders. However, a survey by the Employment Review, found that 64% of employers deploy Assessment Centres when recruiting Graduates, closely followed by 62% when recruiting Middle Managers and 60% for Senior Management. Fewer are using them when recruiting Line Managers, Management Trainees and Technical Staff.

From designing the event to training the assessors to buying all the necessary materials, at an average price per candidate of £311, Assessment and Development Centres tend to be quite costly to run. However, 53% of those surveyed by the Employment Review believe the benefits gained outweigh the costs.

One drawback is the length of time it takes to design the event, ensuring each exercise is measuring its intentions, the length of time that is required to train each assessor, as well the time it takes to score and decide the most suitable candidate. Candidates attending an Assessment Centre should expect to partake in at least one interview, as well as a range of group exercises. The Employment Review Survey found that 77% of those questioned used group exercises, 69% used role plays, 69% psychometric tests, 61% a written analysis exercise and 54% a presentation.

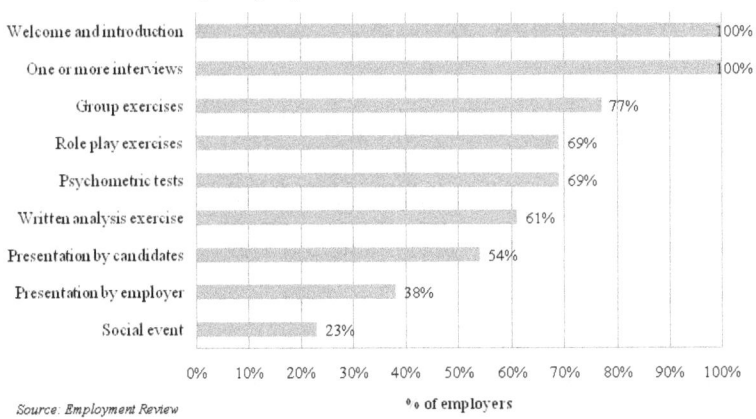

Activities used by employers in assessment centres

- Welcome and introduction: 100%
- One or more interviews: 100%
- Group exercises: 77%
- Role play exercises: 69%
- Psychometric tests: 69%
- Written analysis exercise: 61%
- Presentation by candidates: 54%
- Presentation by employer: 38%
- Social event: 23%

Source: Employment Review

What is apparent, however, is the increasing use of Assessment and Development Centres, for an increasing number of positions. A well designed Assessment Centre appears to be the most efficient way of observing and objectively measuring performance on the job and it likely that this recruitment process is around to stay.

Not-for-Profit Company Case Study

A Not-for-Profit company has implemented pre-Assessment and Development Centre workshops, in a bid to reduce the dropout rate. According to figures, providing this has improved attendance figures, with fewer delegates failing to attend at the last minute. In addition, twice as many delegates attended compared to the previous year. This is because the pre- workshop provides informative details on the relevance and usefulness of the Assessment and Development Centre, altering candidate's perceptions. These have been found to be beneficial in several ways. They assist delegates to feel more empowered, allowing them to understand their own strengths

and weaknesses, through which they can better manage their own performance and apply the learning to the workplace.

Key Learning Points

- Assessment and development centres can be used for existing and potential employees to determine if they have the competences necessary for a particular role.

- Assessment centres are used for selection of new employees while development centres are used for self-assessment to determine areas of strength and weaknesses.

- Assessment centres are said to be the most objective and efficient form of recruitment

- Development centres help employees identify ways of improving current performance.

Useful Hints and Tips

- Due to the potential costs of assessment centres, your company can use them for more senior roles or for graduates who are likely to be future leaders.

- Development centres should be done as often as possible to ensure that there is a spirit of continuous improvement in the company.

- Pre-assessment and development centre workshops that provide information on the relevance and importance of the assessment and development centres can be held in order to encourage more employees to attend.

LEADERSHIP – *Arise Aspiring Entrepreneurs*

When you hear the word entrepreneur, what do you think of? Branson, Gates, Blakeley, Zuckerberg? The issue is that there is no standard definition of what an entrepreneur is or what it is that makes them so great. Perhaps what they have in common is raw passion for an idea and seizing upon that gap in the market. Nevertheless, there are some features and behaviours that are commonly associated with an entrepreneur and certain techniques that they use to start up their businesses.

Future Zuckerbergs take notes!

Characteristics of an Entrepreneur

There appears to be no agreed definition of what an entrepreneur is, yet there are a variety of characteristics and traits that allow entrepreneurs to be more accepting of the challenges that they face. The good thing about these is that they can be learnt. Entrepreneurship has three dimensions:

- **Innovation** which requires an emphasis on developing new and unique products, services and processes.
- **Risk-taking** which involves a willingness to pursue opportunities having a chance of costly failure.
- **Proactive behaviour** which is concerned with implementation and doing whatever is necessary to bring a concept to fruition.
- These are just some of the features that entrepreneurs must possess to thrive and succeed.

The Recession: an entrepreneurial opportunity?

The recent economic climate has posed an array of considerable difficulties for businesses, yet it also proposes potential opportunities for budding entrepreneurs. Starting your own business is a daunting and difficult task and may be borne out of necessity, as unemployment/ underemployment may spark entrepreneurial spirit, leading to the creation of new small enterprises. Whatever your reason for starting your own business, here are a few facts and tips as to why starting a

business during a recession is a positive thing:

- 16 out of 30 corporations that make up the Dow Jones Industrial Average started during a recession.
- Walt Disney began during a recession in 1923-24.
- Hewlett Packard began in 1938 during the Great Depression.
- Microsoft began during the 1975 recession (USA Today article).

These are just a few success stories that have arisen like a phoenix from the fire, overcoming adversity to be an ultimate success.

Reasons why a recession is a good time to start a business

It may seem slightly incredulous to suggest initiating a new venture in times of such economic austerity but here are few reasons as to why it is not such a bad idea.

- **Competitors are weakened**: All organisations seem to be tightening their belts and some may even be closing up and selling out.

- **Product or service must be viable despite the state of the economy**: It is important to perform extensive market research to identify gaps and potential niche areas to enter into.
- **Deflation**: Most products and services are cheaper, including good sales on office furniture and supplies.
- **Buy what you need at auction**: Vehicles, machinery, restaurant equipment, are just a few things available to buy at auction at rock bottom prices.
- **Be frugal**: It is vitally important to track expenditure carefully and to keep costs as low as possible.
- **Negotiate better terms with your suppliers**.

These are just a sample of the reasons as to why turning that spark of inspiration that just won't go away into a tangible and viable business.

Tips for starting your own business

Before entrepreneurs embark on their quest for business world domination, there are a few pieces of advice to consider which will hopefully help entrepreneurs on their journeys.

- **Do what you love**: It is immensely important that you find something that really interests you and that you are passionate about because then you will have the intrinsic drive to succeed.
- **Find a gap in the market**: This could be by developing a product or service that perhaps people do not want to do or cannot do themselves. It is thus important to reiterate the need to thoroughly understand your market to find something which is needed in the marketplace.
- **Start a low capital business**: The key is to start small and build slowly and steadily.
- **Keep your overheads low**: This is an essential consideration for any entrepreneur, either hire slowly or do without if possible.

- **Follow the customer**: Value and listen to your customers, conduct focus groups and research consumer spending patterns as that will hold the key to how to orientate your product or service to your target market.

Hopefully this has provided a few useful insights to help guide entrepreneurs of the future. However, it is perhaps interesting to look at entrepreneurship in action by looking at one of the world's most esteemed and successful trail blazers.

A Master Class from Steve Jobs (Apple Inc.)

Steve Jobs, the co-founder of Apple Computers (now Apple Inc.) was a truly inspirational visionary and here are some of his innovation secrets:

- Passion is everything: Passion is the enabler for your idea to flourish. As Steve Jobs said *"Have the courage to follow your heart and your intuition. They somehow already know what you truly want to become."*

- Put a dent in the universe: This speaks to vision. Innovation does not take place in a vacuum. Steve Jobs set out with a vision to change the world. What is your vision for your product, brand, and your career? Passion fuels the rocket, but vision points the rocket to its ultimate destination.

- Kick start your brain: Jobs believed that a broad set of experiences expands our understanding of the human experience. A broader understanding leads to breakthroughs that others may have missed. Jobs created new ideas precisely because he had spent a lifetime exploring new and unrelated things—seeking out diverse experiences.

- Sell dreams not products: Your customers don't care about your products, your company or your brand. They care about themselves, their hopes, their dreams, their ambitions. Help them fulfil their dreams and you will win them over. *"The people who are crazy enough to change the world are the ones who do."* Steve Jobs didn't rely on focus groups. If he had, they may never have enjoyed iPods, iTunes, the iPhone, the iPad, or Apple Stores. Jobs did not need focus groups because he understood his customers really, really well. Yes, sometimes better than they know themselves!

- Say no to 1,000 things: *"Innovation comes from saying no to 1,000 things to make sure we don't get on the wrong track or try to do too much."* Jonathan Ive, Apple design guru: *"We are absolutely consumed by trying to develop a solution that is very simple, because as physical beings we understand clarity".*

- Create an insanely great experience: Jobs has made the Apple Store the gold standard in customer service by introducing simple innovations any business can adopt to create deeper, more emotional connections with their customers. For example, there are no cashiers in an Apple store. There are experts, consultants, even geniuses, but no cashiers. Apple created an innovative retail experience by studying a company known for its customer experience—The Four Seasons. Apple Stores would attract shoppers not by moving boxes, but by

"enriching lives."

- Master the message: You can have the most innovative idea in the world, but if you can't get people excited about it, it doesn't matter. Steve Jobs is considered one of the greatest corporate storytellers in the world because his presentations inform, educate and entertain.
- The final message would be: Don't give up on your visions! Innovation takes confidence, boldness and the discipline to tune out negative voices. Perhaps the ultimate lesson that Jobs teaches us is that innovation requires risk-taking and risk taking takes courage and a bit of craziness. See genius in your craziness. Believe in yourself and your vision and be prepared to constantly defend those beliefs. Only then will innovation be allowed to flourish and only then will you be able to lead an "insanely great" life.

GLOBAL MANAGEMENT JOURNAL

Key Learning Points

- Entrepreneurs need to be innovative, risk-taking and proactive.
- Many great organisations such as Hewlett Packard and Walt Disney started during difficult economic periods.
- A recession can be a great time to start a new business.

Useful Hints and Tips

- Do what you love
- Find a gap in the market
- Start a low capital business
- Keep overheads low

MENTORING MATTERS...COACHING COUNTS

Introduction

You may be aware of the terms 'mentoring' and 'coaching', yet many fail to distinguish between these seemingly interchangeable processes. The main distinction being that within a 'mentoring relationship', the mentor seeks to advise the mentee, whereas a coach will attempt to draw out responses from the person being coached so that they produce the answers for themselves.

Mentoring vs. Coaching

The terms 'mentoring' and 'coaching' may not come as new to you, yet many fail to distinguish between these seemingly interchangeable processes. Mentoring involves a protected and confidential relationship whereby skills and knowledge is transferred from a more experienced to a less experienced individual. Coaching on the other hand is action and performance orientated owing to its origins within sport. You learn from a mentor but learn with a coach.

Mentoring

The key to a successful mentoring process is three fold:

- Creating a climate of trust, confidentiality and respect
- Exploring and clarifying the issues, feelings and opinions
- Deciding and acting

There are a variety of skills that a mentor must possess in order to instigate a successful and sustainable relationship. These include effective communication, interpersonal skills, active listening, questioning, facilitating, networking, feedback, coaching and counselling. This is a fairly extensive list and shows the magnitude of factors involved within the mentoring process. However, that is why these skills are outlined to guide and assist and should ultimately culminate in a positive mentoring relationship.

Mentoring in action:

Siemens is Europe's largest engineering conglomerate, which currently employs  around 480,000 people in 190 countries. Their culture is one of high performance, and they believe that this can be achieved through effective management of talent. Siemens believe in people excellence, and try to develop everyone in the organisation, not just high fliers. Siemens is a business focused on innovation. This means it needs to anticipate and respond to rapid changes in the external business environment. For example, climate change and the growing emphasis on its carbon footprint have massively increased Siemens' focus on wind turbines and renewable energy sources. Siemens needs to attract employees with the appropriate skills, either by recruiting people into the organisation or by training existing employees to develop more skills.

The success of Siemens mentoring schemes is perhaps due to the fact that they do not adopt a one size fits all approach.

They have a number of training and development schemes. All of which include mentoring. Siemens has three main development programmes:

- **Apprenticeships:** Siemens offer a variety of technical apprenticeships, aimed at school leavers who want to 'earn as they learn'. The training is a combination of off-the job college training and on-the-job work experience, whereby each apprentice has a mentor throughout.

- **Commercial Academy:** This was launched in 2005 to further enhance the pipeline of financial and commercial capability within Siemens. The programme lasts four years and is regarded as an alternative to going to university. Aimed at students who have a keen interest in Business and Finance, the programme enables students to rotate around various finance and commercial placements including Accounting, HR, Procurement and Corporate areas.

- **Graduate Programmes:** The graduate programmes

cover three core areas of the business including; Engineering (electrical/electronic, mechanical/mechatronic), IT (R & D, design, consultancy) and Business (HR, sales, project management). Each graduate is treated as an individual, with their own unique training and development plan.

Benefits of mentoring

Siemens have found many benefits as a result of their talent management strategy. They found that employees were more engaged which translated into a high standard of performance within customer facing roles, which as a consequence lead to greater customer satisfaction. Also, because everyone is given development opportunities and the opportunity to become talented personnel, it has allowed individuals more choices and the ability to achieve their full potential, meaning they are more satisfied.

Coaching

Skills of a coach are comprised of giving feedback, learning to listen and focusing on the types of questions to be asked.

- **Giving feedback:** feedback should be specific and objective, meet the needs of the coach and concern behaviours that they can adjust. It must also be appropriate, timely after a particular behaviour has occurred and the coach should verify their understanding of the discussion.

- **Learning to listen:** listening is an art form. Being able to listen effectively can be difficult, as we all fall victims to bad habits such as not paying attention or interrupting. It is therefore important to be aware of your flaws, to challenge and overcome them.

- **Improving listening:** in order to advance your listening skills, it is important to be aware of poor listening habits, so that you can make a conscious effort to tackle them. Coaches need to actively pay attention by focusing on the speaker and use non-verbal cues such as eye contact, nods etc. It is also vital for coaches to listen to the whole message before evaluating and to paraphrase what the speaker has said so that there is no misinterpretation of the message.

- **Types of questions:** developing a fluid, succinct and appropriate question style is an art form of being a coach. Closed questions requiring a one word response should be avoided as they do not encourage discussion or expression of opinion. Leading questions attempt to guide speakers in a particular direction, planting the seed in the speakers mind, and should therefore be encouraged. An open question format such as "Tell me about a time when…" is much more fruitful in regards to engaging in what the speaker thinks, feels and wants. This allows for further probing questions, to explore issues more deeply. Again, the coach should paraphrase and ask reflective questions to clarify that the coach understands the speaker's position.

The GROW Structure of Coaching

There are a variety of structures used for coaching sessions but the most popular appears to be the GROW model:

Goal: the coach and person being coached agree on the topic of discussion and objectives for their time together.

Reality: in this stage the pair explores the current situation, both the factors and people involved.

Options: here the coach will explore different actions open to the person being coached and facilitate their movement towards making it happen.

Wrap up: this is where the coach will help the employee to commit to taking action, within timeframes and exploring any obstacles.

Case Study: Ernst & Young

Ernst & Young is one of the world's big four accountancy firms. They deliver a variety of audit, tax and risk management services to a range of large and small, public and private sector organisations including many FTSE 100 companies.

Peter Matthews, the pioneer of the business development coaching programme, proposed that a change of mind set and deployment of appropriate skills within the organisation were essential. Mr Matthews indicated that coaching would optimally work when the recipients feel it will help them achieve their goals. The current structure of coaching support was developed following a mapping exercise of skills. It was recognised that the relevant skills were generic (life skills was the term adopted) and topics like effective questioning and listening could be developed in any situation. However, the implemented coaching was to take many forms from supporting individual pursuits to those working within business and service areas, thus using a combination of individual and team coaching. There are now 150 staff members involved in business development, all providing coaching support to help progress the employees of Ernst & Young, to ultimately drive the business forward. Nevertheless,

> Mr Matthews believes the programme will continue to evolve and prove to be an even greater success in the future.

There are various differences and benefits associated with both mentoring and coaching. Mentoring is the most successful method of facilitating learning. It is a tool which benefits all – the learner, the mentor, the team as well as the whole organisation. Coaching is much more performance and results orientated, thus suggesting it is the more fruitful method because of results for the business. Therefore, in conclusion that is why we believe that mentoring matters but coaching counts.

 Key Learning Points

- One can learn from a mentor, but learns with a coach
- Mentoring can be a hit or miss affair depend ending on the quality of individuals populating an organisation.

- Coaching is a more reliable and consistent methodology that delivers significant personal benefits.

Useful Hints and Tips

- To be a successful mentor, one needs to create a climate of trust, explore and clarify the issues and then make informed decisions and act upon them.
- Learning to listen and adapting an appropriate questioning style are key features of being a successful coach.
- Organisations may find that a combination of both paves the way to success.

STRATEGIC ORGANISATIONAL DEVELOPMENT – Approaches and Challenges

Introduction

Organisational development (OD) is a response of an organisation to changing and challenging economic and environmental factors. It is an initiative and change process designed to bring about a particular result. There are three big questions that organisations must ask in the early stages of a strategic development. They are: 'Where are we now?', 'Where do we want to go?' and 'How will we get there?' Developing an organisational strategy consists of constructing competitive moves and business approaches to produce successful performance.

OD Model

Organisational Development can be implemented in three core stages. The first stage refers to surveying and observing the organisation. In this Diagnosis Stage the organisation is directly observing the people and processes in order to determine which areas need improvement. The internal documents, policies and goals of an organisation are studied and employees are surveyed for their opinions. This step helps to identify the problems an organisation is facing and makes the whole process of an OD more organised and structured.

Interventions are the second stage of the development and they can range from simple questions to a whole complex process. Depending on the nature of the problem a specific intervention can be chosen. For example, if an organisation is facing the common problem of skills shortage, then a strategy would be a process consisting of identifying the necessary skills, the skills which need to be enhanced, designing training sessions, and evaluating them. Examples of interventions are mentoring and team building.

Evaluation and feedback are the final steps of OD. Evaluation is undertaken to determine if the expected results are being achieved. Interviews, surveys, and performance indices are often used to evaluate the effectiveness of an organisational change. Finally, feedback provides the mechanisms to reinforce and adjust the planned change efforts.

Senior Management Coaching at Vodafone

Vodafone, the global  communications technology company was an early leader in the mobile telephone industry. With the growing competition in the industry, the company decided to adapt its culture in order to remain innovative and a leader in the increasingly challenging market. A specific aspect of the culture that the company wanted to change was their 'command and control' customs of blame. It was thought that the current culture would hinder collaboration needed to succeed in the competitive environment.

Intervention

Culture initiatives were implemented, including the development of shared values and the establishment of teams and team building programmes. New collaborative management styles were encouraged through the implementation of a leadership training programme. As a result, managers began delegating more and teams started solving problems themselves. Teams began to feel confident in their activities and decisions as managers placed more trust in them. It could be said that some of the company's subsequent successes could be attributed to these intervention programmes.

OD in Practice

The first and foremost step in designing an OD Strategy is setting up a framework for classifying the different approaches to organisational development and then describing these different strategies. The programme should consist of numerous stages such as defining vision statement, mission, aims and goals/objectives.

To define organisational goals and objectives we need to ask some questions first; for example how the goals are going to reflect the organisation's mission statement, or what the long term outcomes of the actions needed for the objectives will be. A vision statement is about what your organisation wants to become in the future. It should be simple and motivate all employees by telling them the future plans of the organisation. The employees should internalise the mission statement and build it into their identity. Around the mission statement, values, and goals there should be structures. Depending on the organisation the above should relate to managers, departments, and teams. Companies whose employees understand the mission and goals enjoy a 29% greater return.

Organisations usually succeed in OD if they entirely commit to the change and development process by embedding it into their cultures.

(Excerpt: Famous Mission Statements, (Facebook) "Facebook's mission is to give people the power to share and make the world more open and connected", (Coca-Cola) "To refresh the world...To inspire moments of optimism and happiness...To create value and make a difference", (Sony) "To experience the joy of advancing and applying technology for the benefit of the public.")

(Excerpt: Trust is one of the top values respected amongst companies, as it can improve relationships and connections).

Main Approaches of Organisational Development

OD strategy should be delivered in a specific way. First of all, the employees should be empowered to act. Once employees take ownership of the change and development process they become more engaged and enthusiastic about its completion.

Moreover, empowerment creates a sense of responsibility over a particular development opportunity. Open communication can help empower employees but more than this it makes employees aware that a change and development is needed by highlighting the areas in the organisation which need improvement. The culture of common effort and collaboration will affect the teamwork and the action towards a common goal. This way an organisation ensures employees are involved in the process together, look at the bigger picture of the problem and are concerned with many departmental issues rather than their own interests. Lastly, an OD promotes the learning in the organisation and learning culture facilitates the promotion of organisational development. If people have a need for improvement and desire to learn as individuals and as members of the organisation then they will enable change and create a better working company.

Challenges of Organisational Development

Numerous factors can influence the success of an OD strategy and there are numerous obstacles that strategists and organisations should be aware of when attempting to implement an OD strategy.

One of the issues is Resistance to Change which occurs when people are anxious about change therefore resisting it. Associated with resistance are negative mood, gossiping, not following the change, turning others against the organisation, replacing the negative feelings associated with change on the boss or other employees, and experiencing stress. Nevertheless, there are certain steps an organisation can take to overcome these issues such as explaining the change process to the employees and communicating change throughout the process, as well as ensuring support is given to employees Secondly, depending on the complexity of the development strategy the cost of the intervention might be significant. In most of the cases an outsourced organisation needs to be re-employed to implement the changes and to review the progress. This in turn is linked with expertise; the change process should be monitored by specialist psychologists and for the success the process should be implemented with a great deal of thought and consideration.

Problem Diagnosis is a tricky part in OD. Relevant departments and staff need to be involved in the process of gathering information. The employees should feel empowered and be able to propose suggestions, and at the same time they should be honest and truthful.

Organisational objectives and goals need to be clearly communicated at every organisational level. This ensures that the staff members know what their responsibilities are. The OD strategy can be defined in line with the objectives to save costs and to make sure that only essential issues are focused upon.

Values and vision establish common goals for the employees and build a sense of belonging and identity within the

organisation. They are essential when considering an OD Strategy as they enable working within a set of established rules. People feel more empowered about the change if it is in line with their own and their organisation's values. For example, if an organisational value was set as an ambition then working towards development and organisational growth is in line with this particular value. Regardless of the costs to them, employees will support the change if it is in line with their values as they will recognise it as an essential step for growth. Corresponding to this should be a leadership that is delivered in line with the values and vision. Any discrepancy between the two may indicate an inconsistency and lead to decreased engagement from employees. Lack of engagement on the other hand is a real issue when it comes to implementing the change process.

Key Learning Points

- Organisational development is an important process in a continuously changing business environment.
- It is important that employees are involved and empowered throughout the organisational development process in order to ensure the process runs smoothly.
- It is important that the process of organisational development is completely embedded in a company's culture in order for it to succeed.

Useful Hints and Tips

- Tools such as the organisational development model can be referred to in order to help with the process and give it more structure.
- Ensure that every employee is aware of the company's mission and goals in order to ensure success.

ABOUT THE AUTHOR

Michael A. Potter

MBA, MA, BA (Hons), FCIPD

Michael A Potter is an International Management Development Trainer, Writer, Speaker, a Globalist and People Expert and has been CEO of MPA Consulting Ltd. and Michael A. Potter International, Manchester UK, for the last 20 years. Michael is one of the leading, non-academic, Global Training and Management Development Consultants and has worked in an advisory capacity for a variety of Global Organisations including, Rolls Royce, HSBC, the BBC, Vodafone, Coca Cola, SMART, NLNG, British Nuclear Fuels Limited and the National Health Services UK.

Michael holds an MBA and a 1st degree in Business Studies from the University of Liverpool UK together with an MA in Organisational Analysis and Behaviour from University of Lancaster UK. He is also Chartered Fellow of the UK's Institute of Personnel And Development. He is a member of the Association of MBA's and an active member of the North European HRM forum, and a former visiting lecturer at the University Of Liverpool.

He has presented at conferences, delivered training workshops and seminars in numerous countries across Europe, Middle East, Africa and Asia, and is a regular contributor to specialist HR publications such as Asia Management Systems (South East Asia) and the Human Factor (India), and many other professional journals. He has recently published his new Global HRM Journal and a DVD "Mentoring Matters, Coaching Counts".

Michael has successfully presented his World Series Paper 2 and interactive workshop entitled "Global Talent Management: Recruitment, Retention and Development Strategies for the

Future" in Eastern Europe, South East Asia and West Africa. Following the success of this paper, Michael has brought out his World Series Paper 3 and accompanying workshop entitled "Human Capital, Competitive Edge, and The Credit Crunch: Global Challenges Ahead". In November 2012 Michael appeared as a key note speaker at the 16th IFTDO Regional Congress in Poland where he successfully launched his new People Matrix Management Model.

Contact

To find out more about workshops, master classes and keynote speaking topics please contact Michael A. Potter on: +44 (0) 161 776 4383 or alternatively email me at: michael@map-int.com. Please also visit our website at www.map-int.com.

REFERENCES

Brenneman, G. (1998). Right away and all at once: How we saved Continental. *Harvard Business Review*: On Point [organisational change case study], 44-54

Capodagli, B. (2010). Pixar's Eight Beliefs that Create a Culture Of Passion. *HRM today*.[Online]. Available at: <http://www.hrmtoday.com/featured-stories/pixar%E2%80%99s-eight-beliefs-that-create-a-culture-of-passion/>

Catmull, E. (2008). How Pixar Fosters Collective Creativity. *Harward Business Review*. [Online]. Available at: <http://hbr.org/2008/09/how-pixar-fosters-collective-creativity/> September 2008.

Dawson, T. (2012). Brand arrogance and the road to redemption for NetFlix. [Online], Available at: <http://www.pullinc.com/brand-arrogance-and-the-road-to-redemption-for-netflix/>

De Valk, P. (2012). Mind the generation gap: how managers can engage with Gen Y. *HR Magazine*. [Online], Available at:

<http://www.hrmagazine.co.uk/hro/features/1075529/mind-generation-gap-managers-engage-gen-y>

Duff, C (2011). Global Talent Management in Action:Siemens-Success through business execution. *HR Zone* [Online]. Available at: <http://www.hrzone.co.uk/topic/technology/global-talent-management-action-siemens-success-through-business-execution/109793>

Gable, T. (2012). Eight easy ways to damage your brand image, lose 1 million customers and $8 billion in market cap the Netfilx Way. [Online], Available at: <http://www.gablepr.com/clientserviceresults/damage-your-brand-image-the-netflix-way/>

Manpower Group (2015). 2015 Talent Shortage Survey. [Online]. Available at: <http://www.manpowergroup.com/research/research.cfm?chooseyear=2012&categoryid=2>

Nelson, K. & Aaron, S. (2012) Change Management. White Paper.

PriceWaterhouseCooper (2011). Millenials at work – Reshaping the workplace. [Online], Available at:

<http://www.pwc.com/gx/en/managing-tomorrows-people/future-of-work/key-findings.jhtml>

Rao, H., Sutton, R., and Webb, A.P.,(2008). Innovation lessons from Pixar: An interview with Oscar-winning director Brad Bird. *Strategy Practice*. [Online], Available at:
<http://www.mckinseyquarterly.com/Innovation_lessons_from_Pixar_An_interview_with_Oscar-winning_director_Brad_Bird_2127>

The Times 100 Business Case Studies (2012). Overcoming Barriers to change: A Corus case study. [Online]. Available at:
<http://businesscasestudies.co.uk/corus/overcoming-barriers-to-change/introduction.html#axzz2PV5riMbi>